Humming

Also by Maurice Scully

Poetry

Love Poems and Others (Raven Arts Press, 1981)
5 Freedoms of Movement (Galloping Dog Press, 1987)
Prior (Staple Diet, 1991; tel-let, 1992)
Certain Pages (Form Books, 1992)
Over and Through (Poetical Histories, 1992)
The Basic Colours (Pig Press, 1994)
Priority (Writers Forum, 1995)
Prelude, Interlude and *Postlude* (all Wild Honey Press, 1997)
Steps (Reality Street Editions, 1998)
Etruscan Reader IV
    (with Bob Cobbing & Carlyle Reedy: etruscan books, 1996, 1999)
5 Freedoms of Movement (revised edition, etruscan books, 2001)
Tree with Eggs (hardPressed poetry, 2004)
Livelihood (Wild Honey Press, 2004)
Numbers (Coracle Press, 2006)
Sonata (Reality Street Editions, 2006)
Tig (Shearsman Books, 2006)
Doing the Same in English (Dedalus Press, 2008)
Work (Oystercatcher Press, 2008)
Five Dances (echapbook, Ahadada Books, 2009)

CD
Mouthpuller (Wild Honey Press/Coelacanth Press, 2000)

Children's
What Is The Cat Looking At? (Faber, 1995)

Humming

MAURICE SCULLY

for Bill
in appreciation

Maurice
Dublin '09

Shearsman Books
Exeter

Published in the United Kingdom in 2009 by
Shearsman Books Ltd
58 Velwell Road
Exeter EX4 4LD

www.shearsman.com

ISBN 978-1-84861-059-0
First Edition

Acknowledgements

Some parts of this book have been published by
Stride, Coracle, Four Courts & Dedalus Press.
Grateful thanks to the editors, Peter Robinson, Robert Sheppard,
Simon Cutts, Erika van Horne, Philip Coleman and Pat Boran.

Flower image on page 85 by Leda Scully.

CONTENTS

HUMMING
[the words]

Song

SONNET SONG

Look: if the coin had landed on its edge making the
spaces to heads and tails the space of all probability
patterns lit up to date stretched to an evanescent blur
(one little thought experiment deserves another)
then *you* this, *me* that – *plink!*

(knock)

If – rock of constancy, rubble of contingency –
(pass the salt) giving the bracket its due, its
space, its elastic content, bustle & itch
(where's my sandwich?) ah on the plate. *Pop!* It's gone.

(knock)

If you dedicate your little book to Mammy and get
a prize – size matters – you know how it is –
a million years of isolation and neglect … as if you
deserve pampering *as by right*. Just write, right?

(knock)

If a strange-looking fly walks across your page
in quick, short bursts, stops, grooms its back legs
thoroughly, you could say: with care, in this un-
believable world: look. At the evidence of literature,
the evidence of art and capital. The evidence of the
evidence.

(knock-knock)

If the Way of Art is a Hard, Hard Way
as you heard some old Tin-Can say (dot)
loud sing cuckoo – grows seed – blows mead
and blossoms the wood now –

If.

If.

If …

Sing Cuckoo!

      [the letter *contend*

             the letter *ablaze*]

If …

Put *that* on paper.
Laugh. Emptily. Good grief.
Is it?

             Knock

Youbet.

Thanks.

Yep.

OK.

Right.

Seeya.

             Knock-knock

Ah yes, you're in an altered state.
But listen: so what? Who cares?
Where's my breakfast.
At 53: tickle me.
Food, fun, money, regularity.

Knock-knock

Knock-knock

Knock-knock

Now yr feet are on the ground. Now one foot,
now the other. The ground. The grass. Yr –
as yet undecorated – bones.
Over yr moving shadow – first this, then that –
little butterflies lift & flit – clocks circling –

> *what the heck – I wanted love – you*
> *wanted sex – tra-la cut the deck –*
> *yr fingers tremble – over what they –*
> *may resemble – in their future – (of*
> *bliss) tra-la – you know how it is*
> *tra-la – tick-tick but what the heck –*

> who's there?

circles circling circuits. Circles circling – take
　　yr pencil & make that call tick-tick
　　　　there's work to do.

　　　　　　· ·

　　Then a stray piece turned up called
　　THE DOG.

THE DOG

　　The dog is barking in the laneway again.
　　Who owns that dog? Do you?
　　Do you?

SONG

Brick glistens a little where a
snail recently slid. Split. Sun
through a dusty shed window
under a tree: as yr pen-tip tou
ches paper a long thin shadow
shadows it to the right. Write
that. Tell it. So. Tapping a
tempo on an upturned bucket as
the village kids danced, screeched
with laughter at this mad whiteman,
a crack of lightning of a sudden,
slapped to the east, tacked then
to the south, thunder echoing,
and a black sky – //flash// – wells.

We stop: the rains had come. Happiness
by time over light equals money minus
dark over hope plus n: honeycomb
of a beginning of an idea of a next
move. Whirr of wings, look up: *I*
have (precisely what you need
elsewhere) the bright black eye
of the robin, sideways, checking,
surrounded by, steeped in, silence.
Your move. (Art's lateral, even if
life's tiny – see?) Bottom half,
13 Across. You open yr glasses case,
place it to yr left on the desk, *tock,*
polish the lenses, put them on, begin.

Who's there?

A rain so light, a
little whisper, leaf-
brush, merest whis-
per, how say it,

20 years

light flickers,
a carpenter's
hammering, a
van's reversing

bleep. Dot. The wind
moves.

Push.

Rippling across
the desert as
ripples on the
sea-floor

sand blown by
the wind up the
dune's slope
to crest

vivid at the lip
slips with nothing
to bind it
down the steep

face in a
continuous series
of tiny

avalanches
inching forward −
a stealthy animal! −
across the plain.

Out on the blank
moving across the blank
in a blank   put hinge in   3 Down/5 Across
step one/step two   a gate bangs in the wind
a drill fixing a windowframe   *is is is*
the wind in the trees   a breath   a
breathing & creaking   oh listen   a
saw!

Teach is *teach* in Irish
& Irish is an adjective (too) in English
in whose house the messenger
arrives to say: (drop)
it's summer: wake up.
Flood cells with brood-food
or lose all larvae *now!*
The messenger is here. A dish of syrup.
Múin é. Nó í.

Look at that!
A Cinnamon-chested Bee-eater. One Down. Three

Across.
Begin.

This just won't do. The First-Surface layer
(op cit) carries the lies we're used to.
Massed beds stitched with precision. Burn.
The second-surface layer we get to know.
Burn. A third-surface I infer. Burn!
The fourth & so on down – dig, burn, dig –
signals that buckle their receptors. How does
that one go, the one about The Simple Life?
Hephaestus Was Here. A feathered arc of water
on the glass. Spaces, joins, wax-dabs in place,
as-if as-if, just so. Turn that shaggin thing
off [turning sharp left at page nine yr right

hand rubs down the smooth spine in a light
automatic gesture:
change gear &]
                    hum numbers to edge out
the impossible, but don't forget: you're next.
Goodnight.

SONG

that
    curlew
call
    that
calls
    through
dark
    over
black
    water
all
    the
way
    back
to
    here
(easing
  geese out
    in a wide V
      in the night–sky
      over a flat sea
      write-right
        wright-right
        write-write
          right overhead)
to
    thread
heat
    &
cold
    to–
gether
    a–
part
    wound

&
 bound
crink-
 led
&
 ripp-
led
 like
that
 makes
this
 strange
thing
 out
of
 years
(of
 ear's)
re
 call
(home)
 ing –
don't
 sing
don't
 im
pinge –
 hum
its
 woven
honey-
 combed
surface
 as
it
 polishes
the

                lens
        by
                which
        clues
                bunch
        &
                spread
        moving
                in
        time to
                here
        to
                        [click
        build
                its
        approach
                across
        memory
                &
        honour
                it
        all

                        (through childhood over empty
                        fields, drumlins, lakes, nestled
                        tree-patches, to your ears at this
                        side of this stretch of water
                        at this point in life now)
        &
                honour
        it
                all
        on
                the
        path
                under
        your
                two

stopped
    feet
placed
    pat
together
    like
that.

SONG

BALLAD

I walked along and what did I see? Tomorrow's yr father's anniversary.
Gull-scream, gull-call. Quietness. Hum of life, hum of activity. Two
sand-grains stick. Water carries the memory. Yr table stands still,
still in its shadow, its worklight, still

ha ha   *ha ha*

Turn the room around and what do you see? Is it yr mother's anniversary?
Who died in a cave of darkness, who died in a cave of light. Tricks
shift. Whose life adds up inside you calibrating its un-code. Clouds
mass, sea flattens. Bangs. A rock falls open. Nothing.

ha ha   *ha ha*

Turn the beach upside-down, what do you see? It must be yr sister's
anniversary? By forces too large for all of us she's drawn into the cave.
Greed tugs a string, the thing is done, it's over. In time and space.
The plants inter-leave. I see. Revolve. Carry me home.

ha ha   *ha ha*

Sink yr desk in the dark. So much for study now. Later, magpies in trees.
It must be yr brother's anniversary. A drill cuts through wood, go & do
what you do in life and do it thoroughly, one circle, then another, the
bees' wings, the drill-bit spins, through steel, then rock, do, go, then
slice, ice, down, dice, divine, die, and die well. Good.

ha ha   *ha ha*

Sonnet

huh   not much
huh   maybe not
a ripple on calm water
((a forcefield opening out))
tiny whisper of rain on a roof a
pinecone   its segments much larger to
one side (species? access to light?) split jagg-
ed down the middle where it hit tar-
mac in its fall from …
I move. I stop. I move again
& stop. One, two. How about you? Do you
see that Greed over there?
Eating at your leg?
A trickle a trick
a lull
knock-knock…

Talents: one highly developed
sense of victimhood
an insomniac nature
patchy concentration
ditto education
2 ears, sensitive, eyes, ageing,
a bedrock inability to earn a living.
Chipped Fortune's Wheel though
giggling
– 2, 3 –
huh   not much
huh maybe not
huh

Sonnet

some paper   space   time's table dissolved
snow melting from an eave   can that be birdsong?

hum of a small plane in the distance   hum of my pen
moving   hum of my half-mind following   hum of
the beginning of the lilt of the song of the way through

pock on a ceramic edge   shadows reflected
angle of giving   angle of acceptance

at yr age: grow up.   at mine: out & down.
to circle a house for a lifetime & arrive finally to
know the tune of the closed door

some paper reflects   some papers accept

is that yr name on the mat on the floor? that key
the colour Aloof   a windowsill catching suddenly
the sun

woven (…) slowly

                    thread (…) by (…) thread

to watch one leaf turn   turn back   my hand
yr palm   whatever skill   whatever lack   a tapestry
of flowers in the mud   unstitching the next step

listen to one tree grow   know the connect-points
watch.   continue.   stop.

A Neanderthal burial site found in the 1950s
in a large cave near the village of Shanidar
in the Zagros Mountains of Iraq contained the
body of a man who had been laid to rest one
early June day 60,000 years ago with bunches
of carefully placed flowers: the first time
flowers are known to have been used in a funeral
ceremony.

Analysis of the pollen deposits which of course
are now all that remain of the plants shows that
the tributes included cornflowers, hollyhock,
ragwort, grape hyacinth, yarrow, St Barnaby's
Thistle …

BALLAD

I was closing the machine when its edge
scraped my jaw. That, between, and then,
this. He said. One two. The next move. Is.
Catch it, take it, keep it, a train's shadow
weaving across fields, mountains passing,
a city, distant, gull-spots wheeling, a child
nearby, at a window, where the world
tracks past, a very young child, so happy,
so taken aback, she sings ... bright barns,
white gables, visibility for miles, an occasional
car casually en route, spider cosy in one spot.
Not much doing, a quiet day humming beauty
permanence beauty permanence

> *packed tight with a*
> *wealth of imagery*
>
> > *beauty permanence*
>
> *pervading nostalgia*
>
> > *beauty permanence*
>
> *remains on the level*
> *of the deeply commun-*
> *icative*
>
> > *beauty permanence*
>
> *rhythms delicately*
> *balanced title poem*
> *a gem*
>
> > *beauty permanence*
>
> *north of Ireland –*
> *frighteningly accur-*
> *ate – richness exuberance*
>
> > *beauty permanence*

Beauty Permanence plc – at night then after
the bees' forage in the foxglove and return
in the dance to the hive – who? – *I* am that
constant upstairs star you spy across the fields
by the river, O –

single whip

play guitar

      a little block of wood
      hard work   good
      tapped against another
      one word   two   curb
      & scrub until   hard work
      too   until what?   until
      you

      unblock a mood a mode a code
      a slap-measurement   then
      what?   cut   number & cut   hey
      one/two   again against another
      tap   with feeling &   that
      a good   tap-tap   that a good
      play guitar   lean forward

(ever so)

white crane rising

      sweeping past

          brush knee & twist – step –

play guitar

          brush knee & fix – step –

step forward

      deflect

        downward

                              intercept

& – good – punch

                    draw back (split) & push

cross hands

lay the flowerheads on the ground in a circle here

                                                    | lay them
cross hands | down here
                                                    | like that

dancing in a woven chain

cross hands

dancing

cross hands

folding

cross hands folding

too …

        .

At Ha Tulo, the little church. Then a wave of ululation
from the women in the village. *Likhomo* – her name means
"cows", bride-price, wealth – grabs the pumpwheel to show
what a vigorous girl she is; slender *Likhomo,* crank-scrape
of the swivelling steel, one ripple, then another, beginning,
then another beginning in its wake. So.

            grasp sparrow's tail

Prize-acquirers know their place *and* the password. Yours
Sincerely, Wasting Away. *Mine all mine,* said the dog over
the bone.

> deflect
>
> > downward
>
> intercept
>
> > &

able to demonstrate that while   & here
                                                            in a circle

> (deflect
>
> > downward
>
> intercept
>
> > &)

while the scent of foragers feeding at a dish of syrup is
attractive to all bees – downward – intercept – & even
more – it is even more attractive to members of the feeding
bees' own colony ...

> brush knee & twist – step –

evidence to support the theory that each colony ...

> brush knee & fix – step –

that each colony of honeybees has its own unique scent ...

> leaf & stem
> here
>
> & here
> flowerheads

BALLAD

(Argument)

My brother is dead. I found him at the end of his bed.
His brain weighs 1565g, his heart 465
the document says & helps me know what a whiff
of actuality feels like from those who know the facts of life.

I am 52. How old are you? I'm old enough to take a knife
to any letter from the Arts Council for instance regretting et cetera
because they know I think by now – now that I'm older than
they are & longer on the job – I know perhaps a fact or two of life.

But wait! It's the middle of the night & time to wake up
I mean the middle of yr life & further along the ledge
past the diggers & set foundations parent birds attack.
You will discover starfish ingesting molluscs & ugly
dishonesties between people. You will have been a poet. Why?

What? At your age start again. From Scratch the dog to Doubt
the cat you stand (or hover) wondering if
you'll *ever* get to know the facts of life . . .

I doubt it thought the cat, me too, the dog, & rattled off
a raga to the neighbouring territories. Grab that knife!
I know the facts are rough. Goodbye.

My brother is dead. His wristwatch laid face up beside his bed.

(Response)

    trees
hiss
    trees
bend
    &
sway
    &
grow
    that
way
    &
this
    the
trees
    whis-
per
    they . . .

. . . but
    do
you
    re-
mem-
    ber
they
    tell
us
    can
you
    really
rem-
    ember
depth
    colour

mood
 mode
fold
 &
grip-
 code
to
 never
be
 still
des-
 pite
what
 you
might
 think
in
 all
this
 space
ever
 open
to
 light
up
 each
twisted
 crease
  tickle of silk
  red tin bent
  plastic rusting
  wrought iron
  gritting a hinge
down derry derry
 light under a door
  who'd said a word
   knock
    burn

&
 on
the
 opp-
osite
 bank
there
 listen

listen
 in
the
 dark
&
 in
the
 dis-
tance
 eyes
pick
 out
white
 flash-
es
 that
app-
 ear/
dis-
 app-
ear
 where
rocks
 stop
one
 black
head-
 land

squat
    on
the
    sea.

SONNET

Duck past that branch as rain slips
from its leaftip & the leaves dip &
shiver then down a bit to the left –
just there – palping a bright mass
to place a cover on each tube (left
right) before the lord god of Honey
comes down to eat yr head off with a
ludicrous weaving dance – dab, fix –
bend light to get it right (just might)
on the basis that (Left Right) places
you inside out anyway at Worm Cast-
ing plc where a career in/Now the wind
blows. Now an alarm goes off in the
Land of the Terrified (with two Mercs

& a plush portfolio), now a white
flowerbit hits ground quietly. The
appletree – its business: listen.

Down a path – where's the gate in this
rotation curve in the dark? – left to right
itself against wells of yellow & violet
yes too messed up but gather each grain
putting them together like this then you
knead the mass so that (left to right) you
can pack tight the tubes &/let's-have-a-
helping-of-Infallible-Truth/stop. A spinning
pivot glinting in its own radiant right-wrong
self-reflective chamber each locked facet
snapping savagery & (left right) there under
glass. Then you might (& for sale of course)
then you might like to – corresponding to
a large reverberating gap – take pause.

   2.
     5.

   3.
     1.

Pick a flower. Put a seed into the
big black
earth.

Click on the [Prepare] button. This
is how a dog
barks.

This is how career paths in love
with the true & genuine
historie

of the House of Prizes dissolve

too.

Now *greedy greedy* go the dangers in
the grass/yellow
on

yellow light yellow on light yellowish
white under
blue/

(step) woke ready to re-work all
of the preceding
minutely

patiently grain by grain woke poring
over the
above

again woke check & again.

A diamond design containing a
bee & a rose
& a

what's-it snug reproducing nonsense mirror
sliver of stillness
machines

that seem to speed up towards the corner
the edge to
returns

the possible the window in the other
wall there across an old
armchair

& homemade table

the sun.

Too. Pouring.

Who are these shadowies keep rescripting
the game &
what

is it anyway? (And having come through
all that to
come

through all that). Prepare yr PhD in Twiddle
Dum Dee let's see
is lava

available? One word for Comfortable
another for Slice-of-
Brightness-

in-the-just-begun-under-the-black-
railings.
In

a tangle of bright fragments ($\neg//i \mid i?//\neg$)
of twist
ing

to the shiver of November in the
temperate
zones

in a time of light breeze
like waves &
half

silence in twilight buried parents
appear disappear
under

the pleating trees revealing a dead
sister waving *as-if* one-
two

as-if two-three – gone – the wind – yr
brother – gone (   ) –
too.

Stop. The wind in the branches. Spread-

ing all territorial dog-talk far: ave wave
ave weave wave ave.
Hey!

Too.

[*Blank*] [   ] One block of wood to/

one block of wood to tap a set
piece
too

taps in the wood in the dark a trapped
/   /to let go a small
a–

symmetry in the dark/   /a trapped shadow
at the
edge

until design returns repetition to the
wood in the
wood

in the wood. Down derry derry. Light
under a
door.

          Who'd said a word.
             Knock.

             Burn.

Water in the tank by the gable falling
into the pipe system of this house
you're living in now – look – a

> son at a
> piece
> of music

around which whispers & heaps a dance of
litter – each crease of old paper – each
scrap of plastic – lids, bottletops, cans –
sifted sell-by dates – circles in a corner,
weaves in a corner on the wind around a
garden's single surviving tree. Pick an
> apple.

Touch a leaf. Take a breath, (& give it back).
World that spins & glistens – dance – quite
right – dance in despite of either side the
symmetry of (dance) & to despite of right
imposed/Stand back stand back, you can stand
back from it now. Stamp. You can cut it up.
You can say what you like but that's no good.
You can burn the papers (stamp & turn), diss-
olve the blocks, explode the pictures – crystals,
bees, what-nots – the stillness machines that
stall, shatter the hammer, manage the chatter,
can the past. [*Hey Mum, Hey Mum – I hurt my thumb
& my gum is numb – Hey Mum, Hey mum – Can you
run some fun 'cause my chum is glum – Hey Mum*]

> *hear*
> > *hearken*
> *hearse*
> > *heart*
> *hearth*
> > *heat*

heath
  heathen
heather
  heave
heave-ho
  ho-ho
heaven
  ha-ha

It is spring. It is evening. It is Sunday.
A little rain. Detach the cap, in time, place
tip to page, begin: move, dance, engage (through
time) to watch a foxglove waver, ever so slightly,
a fly hit a windowpane then arc into the air
& away over the rooftop, one bright dot drawing
a white gash across blue the other way, the
  other way.

Got that.

Sirens iron
one's sense
in flat.

I said
then I said
then you a very
particular matter
behind yr hatch
said
then added
plotting succinctly
& well put
placing something
precisely
into a sentence
with a tail to it
curled
pointed
in the dark
& the landscape
as it is
yr window/my window –
gist, variation –
each pollen-dot –
each intricate tickle
across the face
hah.

Sing.

If you watch him
you will notice
he is watching too
cramping world
down tight

conducting mean
calculations germane
to satiate
& what you will
remember you will not
predict
& remember
that he knows that
& will remember it
& calculate
the times to use it
with care
against you
as praxis
to his advantage
meanly, always.

Have a nice/

Dot.

Sirens waver
& shiver
along the black
upper face
of the cold river
at night.
Here.
Each street
beaten flat.
Rhyme that.

Or
shatter
the mirror
image
of the mirror
image of
the what-do-
you-call-it?
Love?
What?

Language-language-language-language-language.

That strange co-
hesion where
threads pull
isolation
freezing
into place
round one
tight
for riding
out perimeters
that bend &
sway

every which way
anyway
so that
deceit
is Deceit
backlit by
Rules that
mirror Rules
that slur
the rim
as a door
slams shut.
Stilted laws.
Swallow that.
Or cut.

A colleague made
speeches & they
clapped happily &
asked that he say

more of the same
down by the Neander
one day I saw
a bit of old ribcage

& a yellowing jaw
& he did & was
pleased creased
echoes of laughter

& clapping in a
corridor a desert-
ed lecture-house
cleaners finished

brushes stacked
a single wineglass
on a ledge a voice-
mail delivering

through fibres in
space earnestly from
somewhere to no-
one. So.

Grain by grain
dust settles on yr
bookstand. Listen.

Where to? Where from?
Arrows – glints –
shadowprints – the
Dramas, one to five …

On slipping away
you didn't collect
your encyclopaedia
all those years

grain by grain
(yr encyclopaedia)
to keep you on
yr toes you know

how it is (how it is)
the corridors the
courtiers the peering
at life through windows

terrified to touch —
quick to grab — take
care — itching back

to close down & return
to main phase & wake
in a space where

curled dead glass
breaks the silence the
rage the next

　piece of shit
　taken for truth.
　Have a nice day.

　.

　My old friends, the Consequences,
　still doing well: fat stem, tiny
　branches, enormous yellow flowers ...

... enormous yellow flowers

cornflower

hollyhock   ragwort

grape hyacinth   yarrow

*St Barnaby's
thistle*

> the
> dark
>   green
>   touched
>   with
>   gold

>   the
>   light
>   green
>   touched
>   with
> gold

It is hard work
whichever way
you look at it.

From biology
from biochemistry
from the building
trade from the nature

of ropes. It is hard
work whichever way
you look at it.

The rest was fragile
intricate displaced.
From uncertain
techniques from

the tightly interwoven
from overlapping margins
from Exit to Emergency
the beginning was an

explosion of surprise
[despite preparations]
it is hard work which-
ever way you look at it.

Dream leaves; clusters of
grapes; load-bearing domes
immune to the moment of the
wind. From the history of

productive mistakes rain
hammering down on to
the skylight out of the
sky of the wettest summer

you ever remember life's
crystal tricks of light-in-
shadow crystal tears crystal
agreements memory's crystals

the crystalline shimmers in
thought patterns from glinting
side-fragments facetted comp-
letions abstract connections

from process across process
linked & weaving whispering
this–that crossways across
    wavelets

of little bits of trash on the
wash & tidal crash (watch it)
I am *hey!* when clouds break
& sunlight floods on to bright

up-readying flowers beside you
& you look up & smile (buoyant-
ly) – 3, 5 – 5, 3, 10 – into
impossibly calm distance. Yes.

Hard work. Whichever way which-
ever way …

   happiness

  by time   *over light*

equals money   *minus dark*

    over hope
     plus
     N

whichever way you look at it.

BALLAD

SNOW

Snow is one of the best insulators in the natural world.
As layers accumulate the snow matures and forms strata.
Warmed by the earth below, the base begins to lose moisture
by flowing off the tiny rays of its crushed crystals to the colder
crystals of the snow above. Gradually an open space is formed
interspersed with crystals of ice larger than those of snow and
different in shape: hollow pyramids that fuse together at their
tips. Down here in this latticework of interlocking ice columns
the air is warm, moist and still. The light that filters through is a
pale bluish white. The only sounds are the scamper of little feet
or the muffled movement of a predator above. Freezing gales
slam into the forest canopy but down here there is food stored
in the forest earth and seldom any need to visit the world above.

Sometimes, a drizzling rain will thaw the upper snow. When it
re-freezes as a tough layer of ice the exchange of gases between
the ground and the air above is blocked. Carbon dioxide begins
to fill the crystal pathways. When this reaches a dangerous level
the small occupants build ventilator shafts (weasels and owls are
alert to their opportunity in a time of scarcity). Or a passing fox
may catch the scent and hear the sounds that signal the presence
of a living animal below. Or a deer may break through accidentally
with its hooves, causing a little local avalanche. Soon though, the
process whereby the lower layer yields up its moisture to the colder
layers above will start again and in time the corridors below will
be safe again and snug.

parquet

white   wall

parquet

white wall   blue window

parquet

blue window   square picture

parquet

picture parquet

square wall

picture picture picture picture picture

DOOR

… dense clusters of pollen that could only have
come from whole flowers, not random plankton
on the wind … And that symmetry, the arrangement
of the flowers … placed around the body of the dead.

Pollen analysis revealed the presence of yarrow,
cornflower, St Barnaby's thistle, ragwort, grape
hyacinth, hollyhock, wood horsetail. The effect
would have been a beautiful mixture of white,
yellow & blue with a deep green bedding on which
the body could have been laid.

SONG

There is a pen on a notebook on a desk.
Still. Put there. Still. Pen, notebook,
desk.

The paper is open. ☐ The cap has been
removed from the pen. There is writing
on the page. Black. A leaf

falls. There is the sound of water. Where,
where does it, this sound, come from? There
is the sound of wind in trees.

Who's this knocking on your oaken door now? Dear
Other, negotiate
that.

A pigeon moving among branches, calling on the
busy line. What balancing circle holds, hovers,
teeters, just there?

Anyhow.

Hum a tune. Think of when. One, two.

Trimming yr fingernails, each thin crescent, each
time different, *you-you, you-you,* each the
same, each repeating surprise. Follow
the circle of yr wrist-

watch, one circuit, then one & a bit, then one &
another bit, at the very beginning beginning
beginning. Breathe. Three

four.

Can you be as tired as I am? Clap hands. 5/5. Turn
the page, reverse the score. *You-you, you-you.*
Are you quite there yet? Is it alright?

Clap hands.

Insert a little translation here. Clap–clap. *The Precious
Mirror of the Four Elements* for instance.
How do you do. Touch it. Clap–clap.

Stamp.

just give us the money & go
just give us the money & toddle off
just do the job & do it properly & get paid & go, on the dot,
    on the button,
just
Just This Once
just watch me pass the Aperture of yr True Judgement &
    dance in that Tiny Spotlit Slit & stick out my tongue &
    give you the finger then I can sleep the Sleep of the Just –
Can't. You. See. We're. Just getting by?
So just skip-along off. Justice? *Hah!*
But then just as you think
    it might all come right
    the call doesn't come & you – oh well
just give up
just yell
just laugh
just watch these thieves snatch everything & spit in yr face &
    get away with it; just this; just this once more.
Just great. But only just.

        Clap *Water*
              Light
              Flower Clap-clap
              Shoot
              Root
              Seed
    Clap-clap *Dark*
              Water
              Leaf
              Stem Clap
              Flower
              Leaf
              Light Clap
    Water-Water/Water-Water/Water

       . . .

a shovel lies at an angle on the ground
rain pooled in its blade   *tick*

sometimes a tiny insect walks across a
page   two–three   dot

moving branch
                    where a magpie
                                        left

how to wait
                    what to expect

post office notice on an envelope from Japan:
"nothing may be contained in this letter."

SONG

Two palace guards on watch – white gloves, red lanyards – under big
bearded naked hero-sculptures with clubs & spears about to do in
the brains of their defeated under-gods among the hinges & springs.
Stop. Tourists go passing in & out these gates in the sun – *lanyards*
click-click *pedestal* click-click *rooftop chimney-pot bird's flash* click
epitaph click oh click click I was touring the lattice now that all the
little cars were grey ah yes he said she said/hey they said I'm/we've
got a new book out have you seen it? they said. Let's see

$$X_{n+1} = BX_n(1-X_n)$$

black clouds over the bay – porcelain gull-dots that tilt, disappear –
the bus red, the notebooks in your pockets/I (it's about) it I think
they said it's about (disparate, desperate) Splinters of the True Cross,
the rack, the plague pit, the twisting-iron, a Court Progress & the
General Terror, edicts in acid, power, whistle & hiss, maybe a merry
madrigal or two & a bit of be-bop too. How do you do. How do you
do it? Love, death & the rentman.

That wing-clap that swoops from coping, Wednesday, the line
brightly, tightly, its drama come feed [& back] straight out of a
tapestry other side of a thicket, grids, meshes, fillagrees. I had a plan
in a dream on a 3D map, plain as that [& back]. Sometimes, cave in
around there, entering the understreet/flash/yr smile in the black
window in the half-dark giving back the older dog that's had a few
scuffles in its time, but still with appetite I/[&]/sometimes a car [&
back] sometimes a car, sometimes my children, sometimes in sleep, a
little shift, return, turn, a house, a place, a time, a (smooth nectary pit)
hope I (build your nest) we –

weave our fingers together taut it clicks like that/we do. Grain by
grain.

Direct you to the flowers

     Collecting & depositing

Direct you to the flowers

     Implanting their minute fibres

Direct you to the flowers

     The evidence

Printing their pollen-pictures forever on the world

     The flowers

  Walls fall
  stones to-
  gether hit
  quietly then

  disintegrate
  quietly then
  disappear –
  pebbles to

  powder –

Direct you to the flowers –

     Come back then to the flowers –

  pollen –
  nectar –
  shape –
  colour –

Down derry derry –

Dance co-foragers to the flowers –

Collect – deposit –

Find the flowers –
work the flowers –
farm the flowers –

Collect – deposit –

Return – start again –

Directly to the flowers – now –

Now I direct you to the flowers –

Evidently now –

Yes – it is – yes it is … ah.

A web is a crowd of kisses: that's the
password. Or one thin stem, or one splashed
open, or green blue red then air then space –
amor vincit omnia – grain by little grain
falling – that or sun-dazzle & a quick
shoal of bright fish developing sideways
under a keel or crux of a windowframe in
the snow (dot). Did you get that money I
sent? Good. For headache, heartache, a twist
in the tunnel, the scales, must – that must
be the password. Then I woke up.

      a pinecone by the
      desklamp each

segment fit snug
to the next each
carrying a little

diamond at its
centre tipped by
a single nipple it-
self a diamond-shaped

echo of where yr
eye last was all
together upcurved
in an airtight swirl –

symmetry & her
twin sister
asymmetry tenderly
delicately &
forever (dot) in play –

breathe. then breathe
again.

then I woke up.

roses and gaudy
flowers roses

gaudy flowers

roses and roses
and brilliant shock-

ingly brilliant dashes
of/and gaudy gaudy

flowers

where you'd taken
a never-before-
noticed

laneway
among the flowers.
The dilemmas.
In pursuit of
& in resolution.
Sing: *foraging*.

JAM

One way or another it should be said that the soft parts
– waxprint – or nine distinct reaches of the responsible –
the night, Continuity, not looking, quite, it's a long story
& colour – drive the Society.

Go, little book to the soft parts of the Society & nine
distinct drives through odour-continuity looking to be
said one way.

He's quite distinct. Driven. The Society reaches the Responsible.
Another long story the night. Honey dab. Odour book. Said parts.

Part looking through continuity & the way another society
is said to be nine books: soft reaching responsible. Knock.

Part of the night book & a little story about a Distinct
continues to be said to be looking society in the eye. Quite.

One-way books are the night. Quite distinct another nine part
ways said looking: drive, continue, little.

Or another way reaches the responsible honeyfarm through continuity
& not looking, one. One way or another – brim, dab – one way or
another, one way or another.

¾ lb butter
8 oz brown sugar
1 lb oatmeal

. melt butter over a low heat
. stir in sugar & oatmeal
. bake gas mark 3 ½ hour approx till golden brown
. when cool cut to taste
. bring (some) on a journey

For Seven Auditions

That flicker between green blades, a bird's chit-chat,
connecting threads, no news, shadowy music,
floating, waiting to reconnect – dot-dot – disconnect,
smoothly swimming around love's core, pouch, purse,
delight's rivet, fluid and sideways, dancing each shape
into place and the core glowing. Great. *Next!*

.

Throw out the mat with the mat-father might be
the wrong motto for the moment. Hey, what are
you looking at? So for the moment then their motto
– itched on irritable stone – is: *glytch.*

.

Slit the pattern-repeaters, edged connectors,
printed ink-dots that slot Going into Going
and mint a Never-Stop policy for Thin-Ice reality:
here we are – drink it. Spindle. Wave. Each small
piece – it feels like that – each small piece
moving in a child-like direction and to a child-like
destination you can't know. *Know* being already
utterly the wrong-minded pip in this. You bet.
Blue. White.

.

Put your glasses on, see upside-down. Sideways-
through. Heretofore. Take them off: a glimpse is
enough. Life's like that – one, two – a speed pickle.
And a dish of syrup. *Next!*

.

That singular sound humming in the bee paste – look – slips
                                                    unevenly
        then
                falls – crystallized –
        into a collapsed
                        on its silver cylinder
                or drops
                                softly on
to the
        plate still
                ness of a lab table
                                & goes *pif!*

                .

                Between the beaded
                & the non-beaded
                strand light's flat
                pattern moving a
                little to the left
                across a wall over
                a paler circle where
                a clock once was

                two freckles (quite
                round) on yr right
                forearm drip of the
                leaking roof *tip*
                teep-tep top breathing
                breathing at night
                beside me beside
                myself delay delay

                begins with a Long
                Call & ends with a
                Facing Away posture;
                in between is the

Forward Position in
the Greeting
Ceremony.

Proof.

·

Begin go the kitten's paw-prints on the bare board
floor one by one by – of care – by one, of purpose,
of exploration *as-if-ah-tissue!* Yes that's ah that's
better. A plane's lights tilting in silence in the
night-sky. Listen.

-.-//Sing:

One flower – one stem –
sometimes a way in

catches an exit (of
power) but then one

flower (put the pen
down) (there) yes one

flower – one stem –
red shadow-pieces

that flicker I some-
times it's I was or

its exit opens on to
a yes/no twitch (pop

down will you & close it
up) each echoing chip

that multiplies what
little there is to

here: here: one stem –
two flowers – every

any other each this
way that a trace-patt-

ern that slips through
(follow it) one small

stone. One small stone.
Picked up. Looked at.

Put down. Pale dabs of
incense-dust that tap

paper on a windowledge –
XP352 – while a bird's

.

song decides
        /otherwise/
              /otherwise/-.-

But to wake in a world
where everything in it were
stuck in place – grip that
spade – polish that bucket –
Mangle of Incident – Angle
of Accident –

                Tangle of Maximum –

Wrangle of Implements –

        Tingle of Precedent –

              Angel of Evidence –

again & then again – welcome to
this stage-set we call … Dot-Dot.
But to call that hokum home? Even
to buy into it to as they say
settle bring your dust to settle
your turbulence to settle your

rigid amphitheatre of pain … hey.
        Hard work.

        Hard work.

        Close window

        Close window
          to return to
          main page

Sing: close window to return to
          main page.

Oak, pine, juniper and ash grew here in these
valleys 60,000 years ago where in summer the
ground was covered with wild flowers among the
grasses ...

the grains in the cave ... minute dots

drifting in on what we now call "June" breezes ...
a little pale blue butterfly ...

or on the bodies of ... the hides and skins of ...
or

... tiny hollows in a bone decoration ... or ...

by water in a deep recess   here   (& here)

a little ripple I think

Look

CODA

SONG

Take yr wristwatch off and lay it on the bed –
good – its three hands – *haa, ha-ha* & *ha-ha-ha*
circling circumstance under heaven. (Move that
stone over there). I was carrying a little pain
in my head. There is every reason. Every reason.
Quickly getting the hang of a balanced eavesdrop
adventure, then moving on. Minutely. Receiving a
salary. Working hard, backwards. *Dear Upset.* Ways-
through difficult of access because of the/it's
because of the Clarity. Each millimetre bargained
for in the black/white grid between parent & child.
Then a sudden free space. Distorted places between
yr eye & the lens, yr eye & the surface, & yr eye
        & yr mindbits & the world. Or

ganized. Thursday. Human. Once upon a time. Techno-
savages in the corridors waiting for image-hit and release.
Click. Crass. Wit and peeve. So. Oh look – there's
a landscape! A daisy closed over in overcast weather,
its pollen-stock, each tiny ricochet, safe and dry.
And something about¬//¬bees~~too and their recognition
||||| of colour. To see ultra~violet as a true colour |||||||
and to recognize the four distinct primal qualities
of the inner reticulate world: those which we call
jabber-of-magpie, gurgle-of-swallow, tricks-of-the-
robin-under-the-hedge. |||||| I watched Rhetoric crawl
home one night and thought now there's a thing. All
the numerous hinges and springs, you know how it is –
no, no – of course you know ah-ha good. Right, so.
A seam, a stitch, a line of tiny zeros in the fabric

through which twists *this* to *this,* fluid thread, un-
dancing thread, appearing/disappearing, holding to-
gether what had not been, tight, fast, in place,
tacked in, a little way on. Drop by drop, grain by
grain …

POEM

"This piece of paper you have just been handed is …
Keep it. It advertises nothing, has no designs on you,
has come a long, long way, to here, in silence, in the
rain, free. As *you* are. You *are.* Now:
breathe …"

HUMMING

In memory of my brother Brian, 1942–2004.